Dr. Alfreda Emonya Love

HEROES

Published by Spines
ISBN: 979-8-89569-748-1

NIYLA AND DEX'S POWER OF LOVE COMBATS BULLYING

NIYLA INTRODUCES STUDENTS TO HER

SUPER POWER FRIENDS

HEROES
STAND AGAINST BULLYING

STOP BULLYING
Hello, I am NIYLA, the listener.
LOVE

LOVE
I'm DEX. I HELP OTHERS.
STOP BULLYING

STOP BULLYING
I'm Valerie.
I value others.
LOVE

LOVE
I'm Everett,
Everyone
is valued.
STOP
BULLYING

My name is **Dex.** I take care of other's feelings.
My name is **Sadie.** I am sad.

Hello, my name is Niyla and I'm your listening ear!
I feel sad.

I'm Valeria and I value others.
I'm being bullied. Please help me!

My name is Everett and I value others. The Love Team can help you!
How can you help us?

WE COMBAT FEELINGS BY:

LISTENING TO OTHERS VALUING EVERYONE

LETS ANSWER SOME QUESTIONS

1. List some good values that we need to have.

2. Which good values do you have?

3. Which good values do your friends have?

4. How do you help others?

5. What does being kind mean to you, and how can you show kindness to others?

6. If you see someone being treated unfairly, what could you do to help?

7. What are some ways you can show love to your family and friends?

NOW . . . LET'S COLOR OUR HEROES!

STAND AGAINST BULLYING

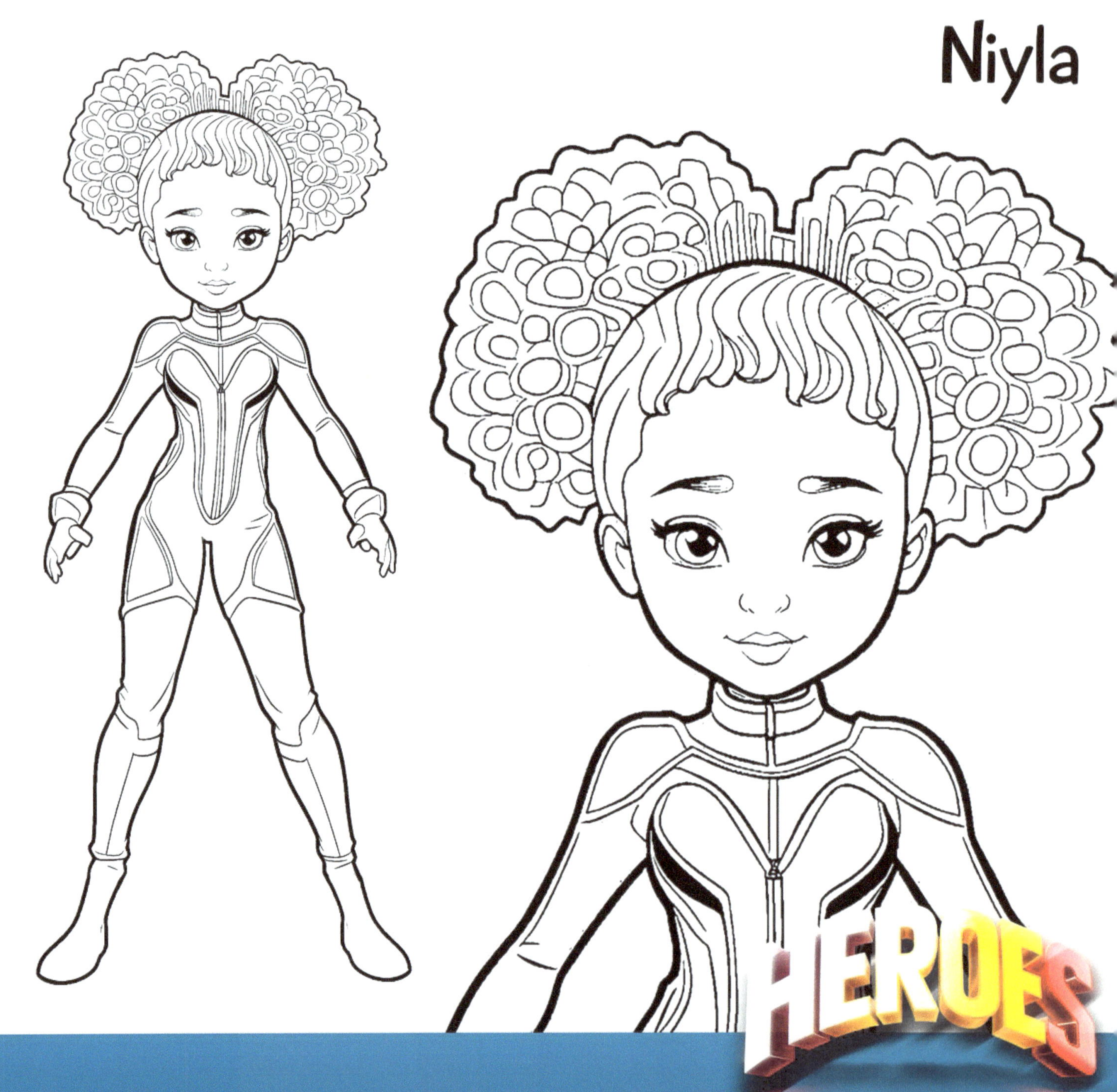

Dex
HEROES

STAND AGAINST BULLYING

STAND AGAINST BULLYING

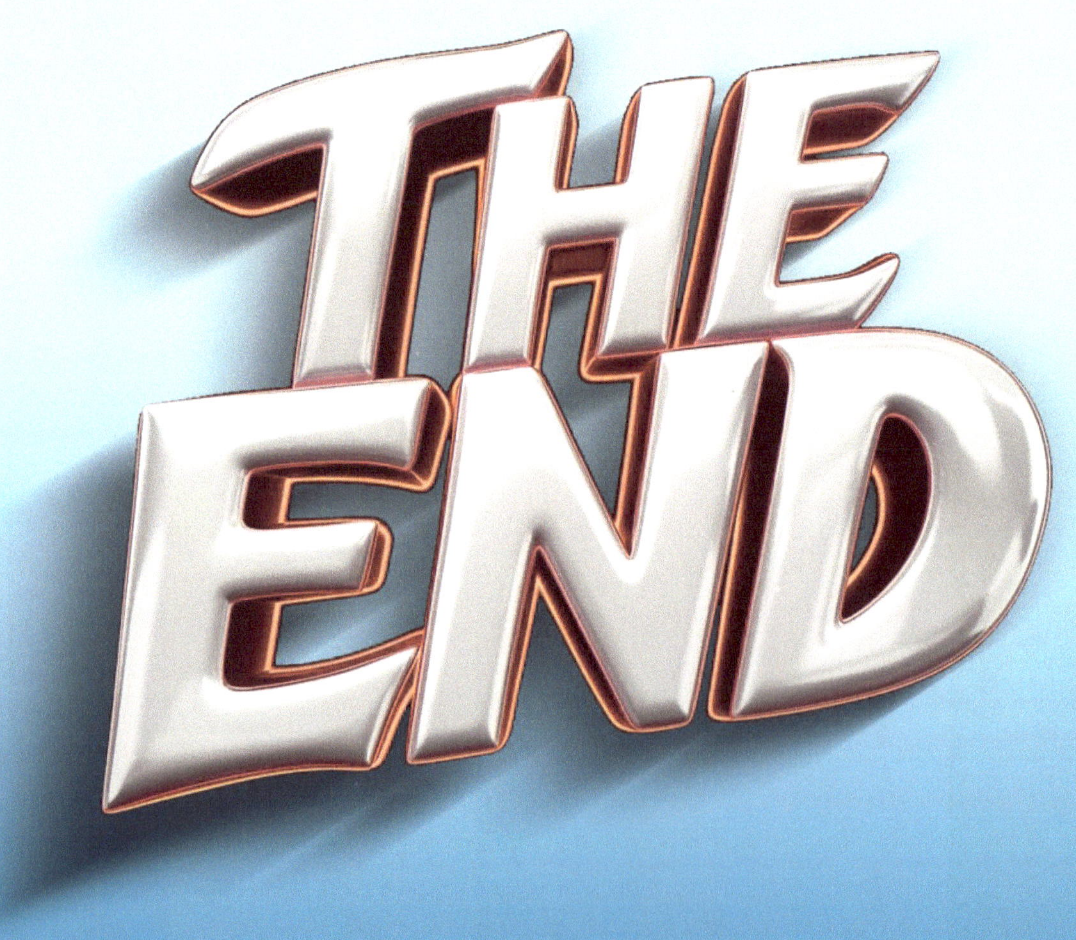
THE
END

ABOUT AUTHOR

Dr. Love is writing children's books to promote literacy and raise funds to build world-class pre-schools in the **United States** and **Africa.** Love has more than 20 years of service in education and believes all students should have strong literacy skills to be successful in school. Each proceed goes towards the vision of building world-class pre-schools

www.ingramcontent.com/pod-product-compliance
Lightning Source LLC
LaVergne TN
LVHW071227160826
845679LV00003B/920
9798895697481